Julia Rothman's

NATURE
ANATOMY
ACTIVITY BOOK

YOU CAN FIND ALL THESE NATURAL THINGS IN THIS BOOK

But first, how many of them can you identify before you turn the page? Write the names in the blanks. Give yourself one point for each one you know and note the total in the first box below.

As you do all the other puzzles in the book, give yourself a point for each blank you fill in, then put your grand total in the second box.

SCORE BEFORE DOING BOOK

SCORE AFTER DOING WHOLE BOOK

Are you a GREENIE
or a SUPREME MASTER NATURALIST?

1-5 POINTS GREENIE
6-10 POINTS TREE HUGGER
11-15 POINTS ANIMAL APPRECIATOR
16-24 POINTS EXPERT CONSERVATIONIST
25 POINTS SUPREME MASTER NATURALIST

Over many eons, the movement of tectonic plates under the earth's surface has created many different landforms.

Read the definitions, then draw a line from each landform to its picture.

archipelago
a cluster or chain of islands

cataract
a powerful waterfall

canyon
a deep valley carved by rivers over a long time

isthmus
a narrow bridge of land connecting two larger land masses across a body of water

delta
an area of sediment and silt deposited at the mouth of a river

plateau

a massive area
of elevated flat terrain

col

the lowest point
between two peaks
of a mountain ridge

arête

a thin ridge of rock left
between the erosion
paths of two parallel glaciers

mesa

a small area of
elevated arid land

butte

a very small area
of raised land
with steep sides

GIANT DESERT SCORPION

ATLANTIC HORSESHOE CRAB

ECHINASTER SEA STAR

BOTTLENOSE DOLPHIN

OYSTERCATCHER

Happy in Their Habitat

A habitat is the kind of environment where an animal makes its home. Above and below are two very different habitats.

Draw a line from the animal to the habitat it belongs to.

CACTUS WREN

LEOPARD LIZARD

DWARF SEAHORSE

HERMIT CRAB

RAINBOWS

The familiar multicolored arc of a rainbow is one of nature's most striking phenomena. Light from the sun may look white or yellow, but it is actually a combination of many colors. Rainbows are formed by light refracting and reflecting through tiny water droplets in the air.

Imagine a rainbow in this landscape and draw or paint it here.

MAKE IT:
YOUR OWN FOSSILS

Fossils are the impressions of ancient animals or plants preserved in sedimentary rock. You can make modern fossils with natural objects that you find around you.

What You'll Need:
- shells, acorns, or other seeds, pieces of stick or bark, or other small, hard objects
- air-dry clay
- rolling pin
- drinking glass

Trilobite from Marjum Formation in Millard County, Utah

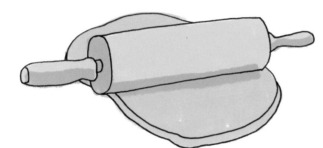

1. Use the rolling pin to roll a lump of clay into a slab 1/2 inch thick.

2. Press nature objects firmly into the clay, about 3 inches apart from each other. Remove each object carefully to preserve a sharp impression.

3. Use the glass to cut a circle around each impression. Let dry completely.

MINERALS ARE...

solid firm and stable in their form

crystalline the tiny atoms that comprise them are arranged in an orderly structure

naturally occurring not made by humans or animals

inorganic not made of any living material

There are twelve objects below. Can you find the six that are minerals? Circle the objects that meet the criteria.

Rhodochrosite

Hematite

Red Mulberry

Turquoise

Salmon Eggs

Hen of the Woods Mushroom

Magma

Quartz Crystal

Copper

Scaly Worm Shell

Halite or Rock Salt

Harlequin Cabbage Bug

CIRRUS
CIRROCUMULUS
CIRROSTRATUS
ALTOCUMULUS
ALTOSTRATUS
STRATOCUMULUS
NIMBOSTRATUS
STRATUS
CUMULUS
CUMULONIMBUS

Which clouds do you see?

Different types of clouds can help you predict
the weather. For example, a towering cumulonimbus
cloud often means a storm is coming.

Use the next page to create a cloud diary.
You can draw the clouds you observe daily in the boxes
and keep notes about them below the drawings.

My Cloud Diary

Date and time:

Kind of cloud:

Notes:

Date and time:

Kind of cloud:

Notes:

Date and time:

Kind of cloud:

Notes:

Date and time:

Kind of cloud:

Notes:

BINOCULAR EYES

Pretend you are using binoculars to look at the creatures and plants that live in and around a pond. Draw a line from the details in the circles to where you find them in the larger picture.

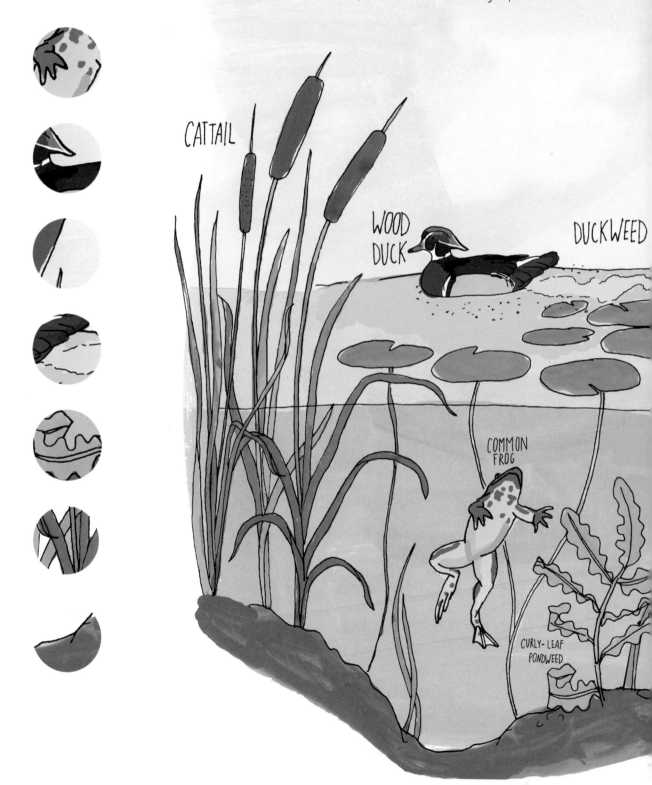

CATTAIL

WOOD DUCK

DUCKWEED

COMMON FROG

CURLY-LEAF PONDWEED

GREAT
EGRET

FRAGRANT WATER LILY

LARGE-LEAF
PONDWEED

YELLOW
PERCH

PICTURING THE NIGHT SKY

For thousands of years, humans have sought meaning in the patterns they have found in the stars. Constellations are images suggested by groups of prominent stars in the night sky. Though the stars of a single constellation appear to be close together, they are usually many light-years apart.

Here are two constellations with drawings of the animals they are named after:

Ursa Major
THE GREAT BEAR

Vulpecula
LITTLE FOX

Can you imagine a hare when looking at this constellation? Draw the hare around the star grouping.

Lepus
THE HARE

MAKE IT:
CONSTELLATIONS YOU CAN EAT

After an evening of stargazing, make an edible constellation of something you found in the night sky. You could use a guidebook for inspiration or even make up a few constellations of your own. Just don't eat too many stars!

What You'll Need:
- mini-marshmallows
- toothpicks and thin skewers
- black paper, chalk or marker, and white glue (optional)

1. Connect the marshmallow stars with toothpicks or skewers to create your constellation. Break the toothpicks and skewers if you need them to be shorter.

2. Instead of eating your constellation, you can glue it to a sheet of black paper. Label individual stars and write the name of the constellation.

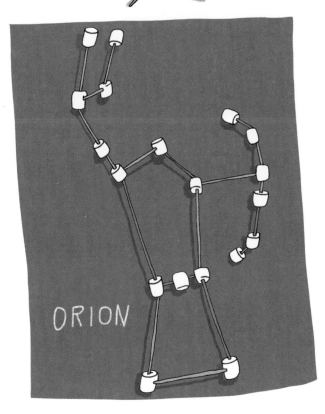

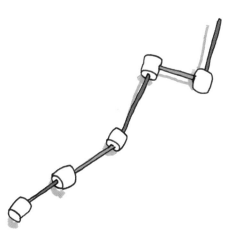

DID YOU KNOW THAT ALL SNOWFLAKES ARE UNIQUE?

A snowflake's shape is determined by temperature and humidity. At low temperatures inside a cloud, water vapor crystallizes directly into solid ice. These tiny ice crystals keep growing until they are heavy enough to fall from the clouds as snowflakes.

As a crystal grows, the molecules do not stack together with perfect regularity. Each falling snowflake travels its very own path through many different microclimates, resulting in a different-shaped arrangement of crystals.

Use the space below to design your own unique snowflakes.

Let It Snow

Can you fill in the 4 X 4 grid below, so all the letters of the word S-N-O-W appear in each row and column only once?

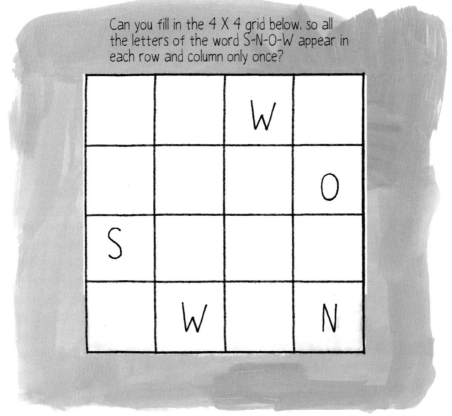

If you look closely, all these snowflakes are different except one pair. Can you find and circle the two snowflakes that are exactly the same?

MAKE IT:
PHASES OF THE MOON MOBILE

Have you noticed that the moon seems to change shape every night? That's because our view of it changes depending on the positions of the moon and sun. Every month, the moon cycles through eight phases as the earth moves around the sun.

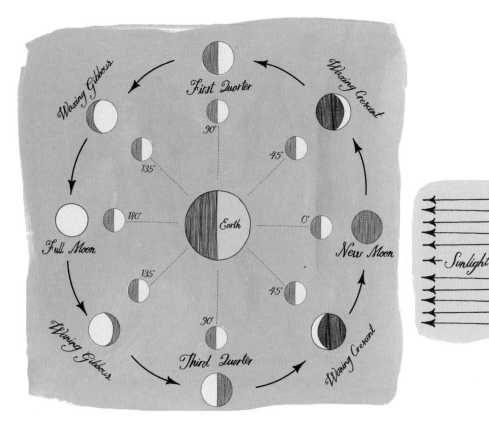

Create a mobile that shows the phases of the moon.

What You'll Need:
- pencil
- drinking glass
- white and black construction paper
- scissors
- glue stick
- lightweight string
- stick or dowel about 2 feet long
- masking tape

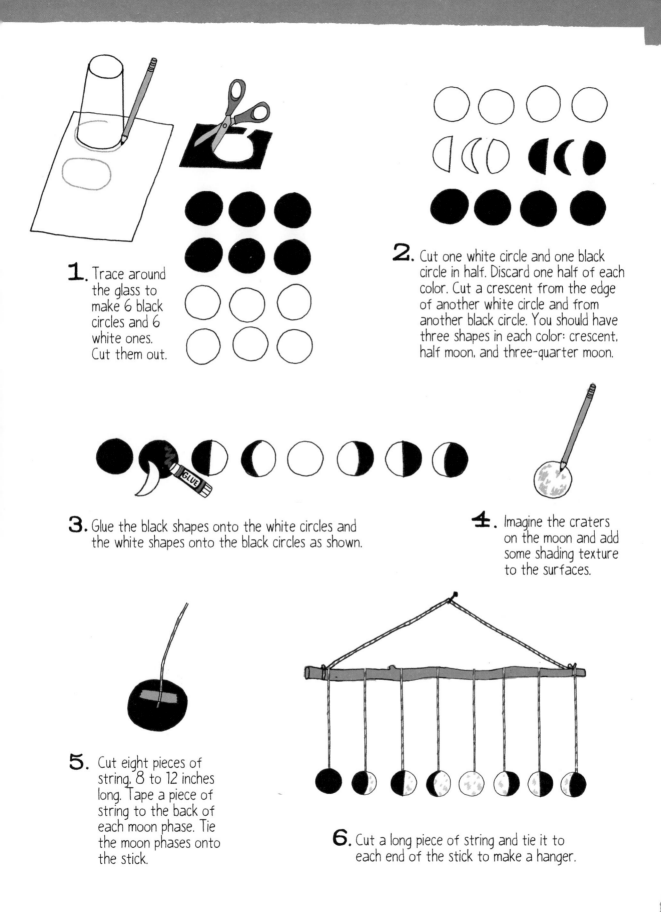

1. Trace around the glass to make 6 black circles and 6 white ones. Cut them out.

2. Cut one white circle and one black circle in half. Discard one half of each color. Cut a crescent from the edge of another white circle and from another black circle. You should have three shapes in each color: crescent, half moon, and three-quarter moon.

3. Glue the black shapes onto the white circles and the white shapes onto the black circles as shown.

4. Imagine the craters on the moon and add some shading texture to the surfaces.

5. Cut eight pieces of string, 8 to 12 inches long. Tape a piece of string to the back of each moon phase. Tie the moon phases onto the stick.

6. Cut a long piece of string and tie it to each end of the stick to make a hanger.

COLORFUL FLOWER NAMES

Combine the circled letters from these flower names to spell the
colorful parts of a flower that attract pollinators.

Baby _(_)U E Eyes

W _ _(_)E Heather

Fire (_)_ _ _ K

B L (_)_ _ _ Eyed Susan

(_)_ _ _ _ _ L E T Pimpernel

Spotted Winter_ _ _(_)E N

(_) (_) (_) (_) (_) (_)
_ _ _ _ _ _

LADYBUG LANES

Follow each ladybug on its winding journey through the grass. When you find the corresponding ladybug, draw the same number of spots on its back.

ANATOMY OF A BEE

Match the body parts in the chart below with the image.
Label the image by writing the correct numbers on the lines.

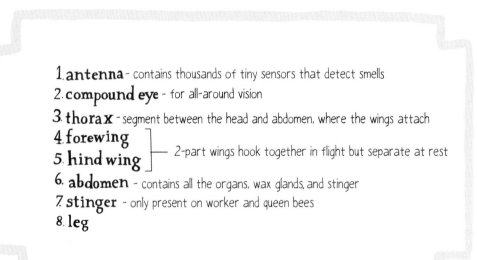

1. **antenna** - contains thousands of tiny sensors that detect smells
2. **compound eye** - for all-around vision
3. **thorax** - segment between the head and abdomen, where the wings attach
4. **forewing**
5. **hind wing** ⎦ — 2-part wings hook together in flight but separate at rest
6. **abdomen** - contains all the organs, wax glands, and stinger
7. **stinger** - only present on worker and queen bees
8. **leg**

MAKE A BEELINE

Honeybees create structures of hexagonal wax cells called honeycombs, where they store their honey and larvae.

Can you help the honeybee through the honeycomb maze?

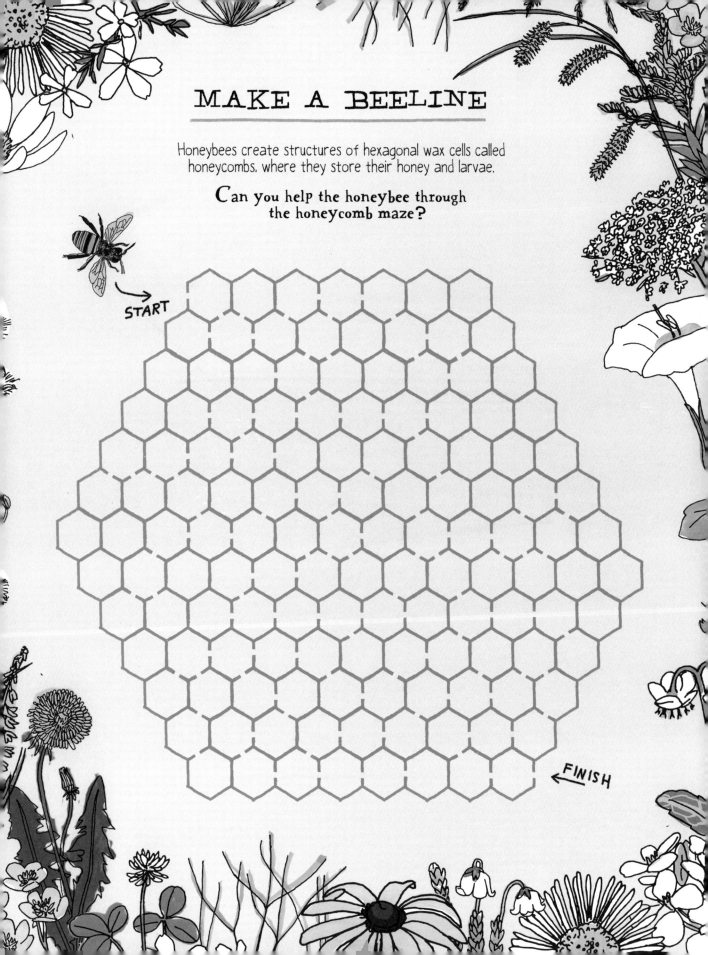

START

FINISH

COLORFUL BUTTERFLIES

Look at the patterns of the butterflies below, and color in the blank wings. Try to match the color and pattern of the other half.

Spicebush Swallowtail

California Dogface

Theona Checkerspot

Malachite

Buckeye

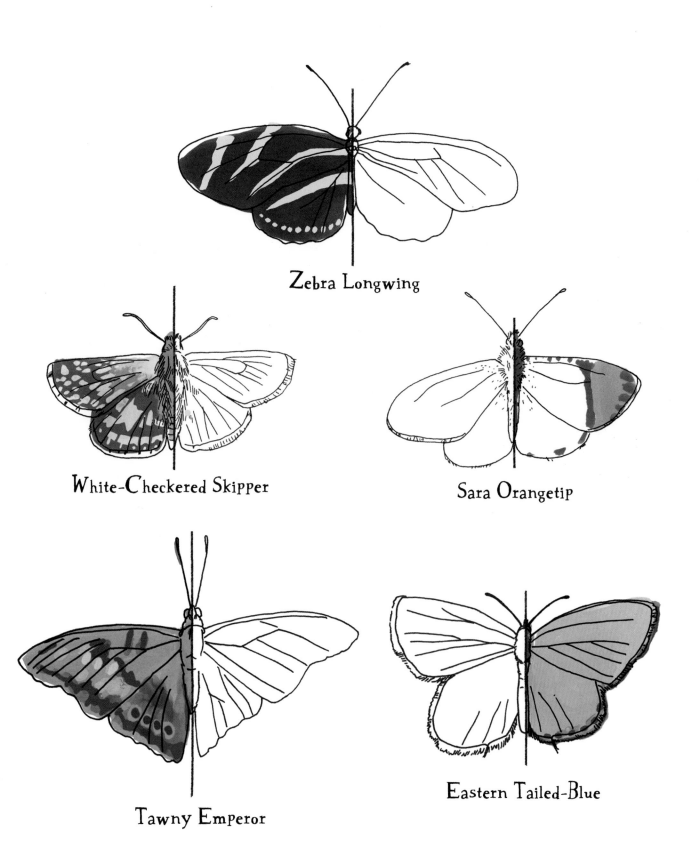

Zebra Longwing

White-Checkered Skipper

Sara Orangetip

Tawny Emperor

Eastern Tailed-Blue

Metamorphosis

The life cycle of a butterfly has four stages:
1. egg   **2.** larva (caterpillar)   **3.** pupa (chrysalis)   **4.** adult

Label the life cycle of each butterfly by writing the
correct number next to each stage.

Baltimore

Long-tailed Skipper

Monarch

HOW MUCH DO YOU KNOW ABOUT MOTHS?

White-Lined Sphinx

Moths are in the same family (Lepidoptera) as butterflies but there are many more species of moths in the world than there are butterflies.

Here's some more information about moths. When you've read it all, turn the page to take a quiz and see how much you've learned.

- Butterflies are typically active during the day, while most moths are active at night. They navigate by the light of the moon, which is why they gather around outdoor lights at night.

- Instead of smooth antennae with little knobs at the tips, moths have feathery antennae.

- When resting, moths usually spread their wings instead of holding them upright.

Colona

- Moths are pollinators, just like butterflies and bees. They feed on a wide variety of plants.

- Moth caterpillars often have hairy or spiky bodies.

- To change into adults, moth caterpillars create cocoons, spun from silk. Butterfly caterpillars form a chrysalis from their own skin.

- Most male moths use scent to find females to mate with. Some of them can smell a female moth from 30 miles away!

A POP QUIZ ON MOTHS

Take this quiz to see how much you learned about moths on the previous page. For each statement, circle T for TRUE or F for FALSE.

T or F   Moths navigate using moonlight.

T or F   Moths are more rare than butterflies.

T or F   Moths like flowers.

T or F   Moth caterpillars can be hairy.

T or F   Moths sleep all night.

T or F   Moths have no antennae.

T or F   Moths make a cocoon spun from silk.

T or F   Moths hide from light.

T or F   Moths teach butterflies how to fly.

T or F   Moths can smell things from hundreds of miles away.

T or F   Moths eat only spiders.

Luna

Regal

Rosy Maple

Hummingbird Clearwing

MAKE IT:
BUTTERFLY CUTOUTS

Make a chart to learn the shapes and other defining characteristics of these different families of butterflies that are found across North America.

What You'll Need:
- 4 sheets of paper, each a different color
- piece of poster board
- scissors
- glue
- markers

Swallowtails
long tails on the hind wings

Brushfoots
the two front legs are smaller than the other four

Whites and sulphurs
usually white or yellow

Skippers
thick body, usually brown or gray

1. Fold a piece of colored paper in half.

2. Using the black images to the right as a guide, draw one pair of wings along the folded edge of the paper.

3. Follow the drawing to cut out the butterfly. When you unfold the paper, both pairs of wings will be the same. Repeat with the remaining butterfly shapes, using a different color paper for each one.

4. Glue the shapes to the poster board and label them.

BUTTERFLY SHAPES

SWALLOWTAILS

BRUSHFOOTS

WHITES + SULPHURS

SKIPPERS

5. Use markers to add the body and antennae and any other details you like.

GRAPH A PARK

How much nature can you find in your backyard or a local park? Head outside and start recording. Starting at the bottom of the chart, color in a square for each species (type) of plant or animal you see. What does your finished graph show you saw the most of?

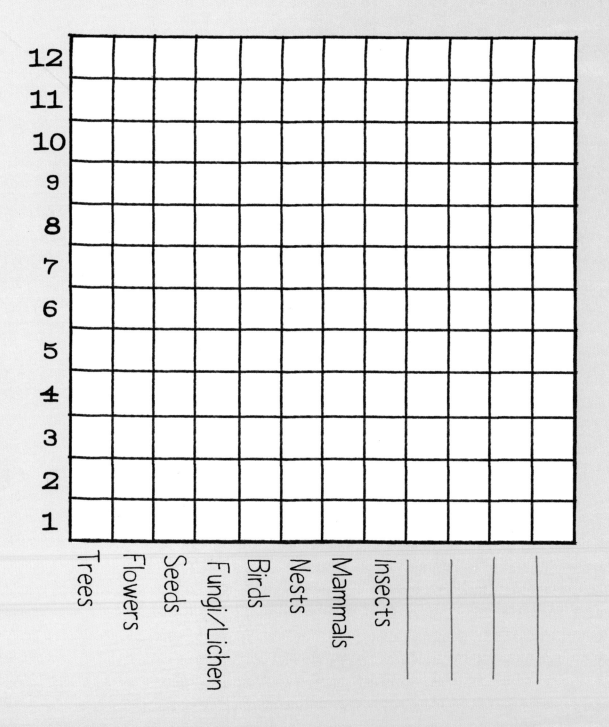

Trees Flowers Seeds Fungi/Lichen Birds Nests Mammals Insects

THESE INSECTS ARE BUGGY

Can you unscramble the letters to figure out the names of these insects?
Write the names in the spaces below each one.

ytakddi

- - - - - - - - -

conrsoip

- - - - - - - - -

gnayipr mtasni

- - - - - - - - -

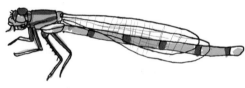

sledmalyf

- - - - - - - - -

otpaot etelbe

gats tlebee

- - - - - - - - -

sppsahegorr

dlayugb

- - - - - - - - -   - - - - - - - - -

Spectacular Spiders

All spiders have eight legs, but these are missing some of theirs.
Figure out how many are missing and draw new ones so that each spider has eight legs again.

banded garden spider   black widow   wolf spider   arrow-shaped micrathena

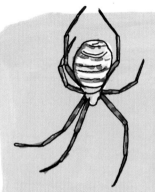

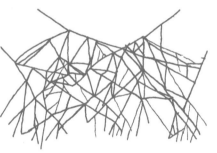

triangle web   cobwebs   funnel-shaped web

Check out the different webs shown above.
Now pretend to be a spider and
create your own web between the two grass stems.

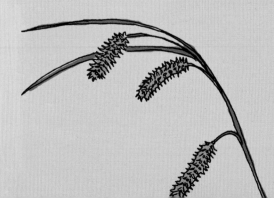

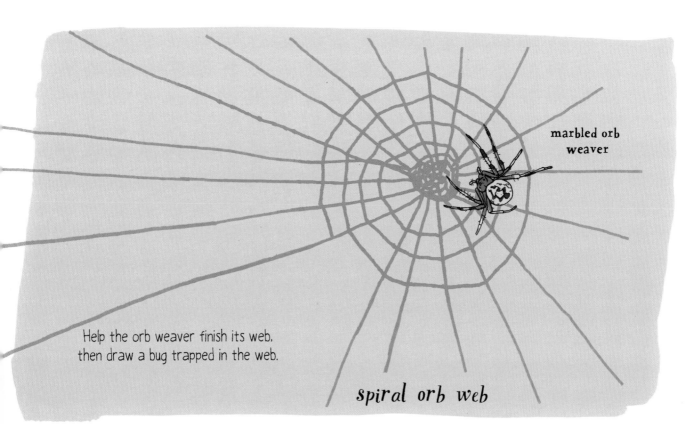

marbled orb
weaver

Help the orb weaver finish its web.
then draw a bug trapped in the web.

spiral orb web

The goldenrod spider camouflages
itself on yellow flowers like
goldenrod, sunflowers, and some
daisies. By blending into its
background, the spider can hide
from predators while waiting to
pounce on prey of its own.

Color the flower yellow so the
spider is camouflaged.

HOW TO DRAW AN ANT

1. Use a pencil to lightly sketch three shapes for the head, thorax, and abdomen.

2. Add the femurs (tops of the legs) and the bases of the antennae.

3. Add the tibia (middle parts of the legs) and the rest of the antennae.

4. Add the tarsi (the ends of the legs). Draw the eyes and mandibles (jaws). Add some lines on the abdomen.

5. Use a pen to go over the lines, then erase any pencil lines that remain.

6. Color in the ant.

Now You Try ↳

ANT

GET TO WORK, ANT!

Ants use their strong mandibles (jaws) to dig underground nests with many chambers connected by tunnels. The chambers are used as nurseries for eggs and larvae and for storing food. As the colony grows, the ants must make their nest bigger.

Pretend you are a worker ant.

Draw some more tunnels and chambers for this nest. Don't forget to add more ants, as well as eggs and food in the chambers.

food

eggs

Tree Shapes

Trees come in many different shapes. Some are rounded and some have pointy tops.

Look at the pattern of trees in each line. Figure out what shape should come next in the pattern and draw it in the blank space.

PYRAMIDAL   CONICAL   COLUMNAR   BROAD   VASE

ROUNDED   OPEN   IRREGULAR   WEEPING

How many of these tree shapes can you find outside?

ANATOMY OF A
DECIDUOUS TREE

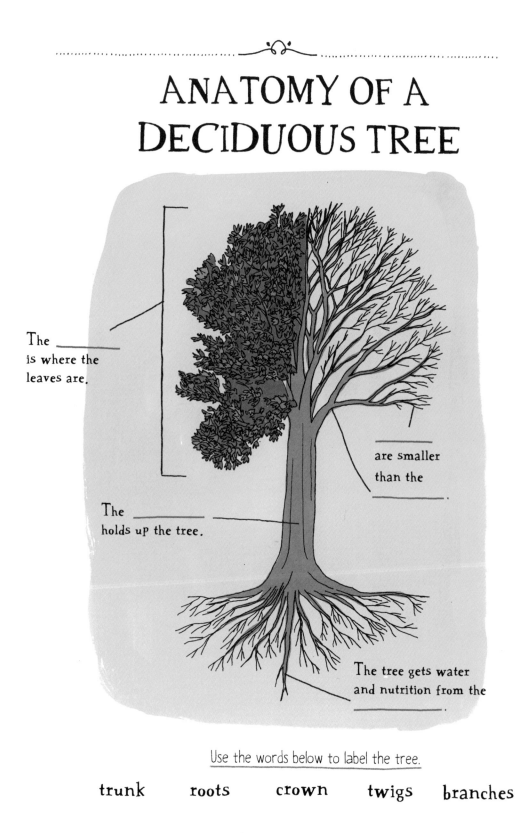

The _____ is where the leaves are.

are smaller than the _____.

The _____ holds up the tree.

The tree gets water and nutrition from the _____.

Use the words below to label the tree.

trunk   roots   crown   twigs   branches

DON'T LEAF IT BEHIND

Like trees, leaves come in many different shapes. Look at the shapes of the leaves below and draw the other half of each one. Try to match the margin (the edges) and the venation (pattern of the veins), then color it in.

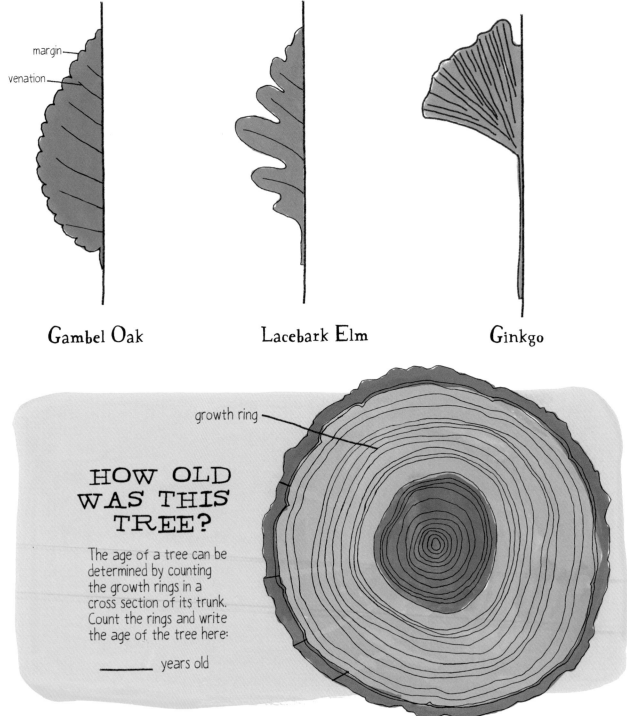

margin

venation

Gambel Oak

Lacebark Elm

Ginkgo

growth ring

HOW OLD WAS THIS TREE?

The age of a tree can be determined by counting the growth rings in a cross section of its trunk. Count the rings and write the age of the tree here:

_____ years old

There are 27 tree names hidden in this word search. How many can you find? Search vertically, horizontally, and diagonally. Circle each one you find, then cross it off the list.

Oak

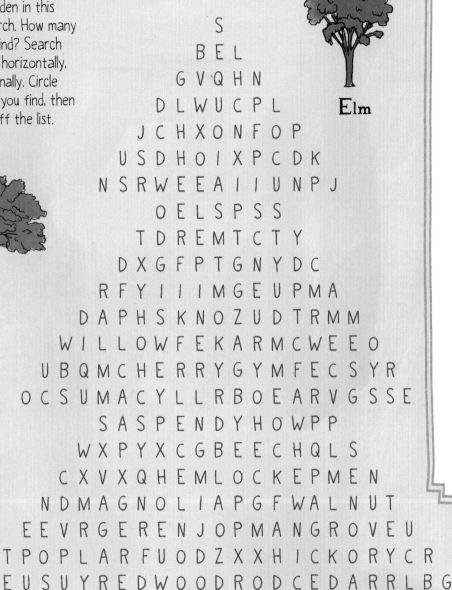

Elm

Birch

Willow

Mangrove

```
                    S
                  B E L
                G V Q H N
              D L W U C P L
            J C H X O N F O P
          U S D H O I X P C D K
        N S R W E E A I I U N P J
            O E L S P S S
          T D R E M T C T Y
        D X G F P T G N Y D C
      R F Y I I I M G E U P M A
    D A P H S K N O Z U D T R M M
  W I L L O W F E K A R M C W E E O
U B Q M C H E R R Y G Y M F E C S Y R
O C S U M A C Y L L R B O E A R V G S S E
    S A S P E N D Y H O W P P
  W X P Y X C G B E E C H Q L S
C X V X Q H E M L O C K E P M E N
  N D M A G N O L I A P G F W A L N U T
E E V R G E R E N J O P M A N G R O V E U
  T P O P L A R F U O D Z X X H I C K O R Y C R
P E U S U Y R E D W O O D R O D C E D A R R L B G
              G B A
              W I S
              O R H
              O C D
              D H A
              O A K
```

ASH
ASPEN
BEECH
BIRCH
CEDAR
CHERRY
CHESTNUT
CYPRESS
DOGWOOD
ELM
GINKGO
HEMLOCK
HICKORY
LOCUST
MAGNOLIA
MANGROVE
MAPLE
OAK
PINE
POPLAR
REDWOOD
SEQUOIA
SUMAC
SWEETGUM
SYCAMORE
WALNUT
WILLOW

Black Locust

MY SEED DISCOVERIES

Have you ever noticed how many different kinds of seeds trees make? Use these pages to catalog your observations. Draw the seeds, pods, and cones that you find, or take pictures and glue them in.

White Spruce

Red Alder

Date:

Kind of seed:

Notes:

Date:

Kind of seed:

Notes:

Box Elder

Date:

Kind of seed:

Notes:

Date:

Kind of seed:

Notes:

Ohio Buckeye

Pecan

Bur Oak

Slippery Elm

Date:

Kind of seed:

Notes:

Date:

Kind of seed:

Notes:

Date:

Kind of seed:

Notes:

Date:

Kind of seed:

Notes:

A-MAZING MYCELIUM

Fungi absorb nutrients through vast underground networks of white, branching threads called mycelium. Hidden in the soil, and sometimes mistaken for roots, mycelium is actually the proper body of a fungus.

Now imagine you are the tiniest burrowing insect lost in a maze of mycelium, and try to get through.

START→

FINISH
←

What's on that ROTTING LOG?

A dead tree on the forest floor may not look like much, but the decomposing wood hosts a party of plant and animal life.

Use the words below to label what's on the rotting log.

ferns   ivy   grasses   lichen   centipede   fungi   moss   mushroom

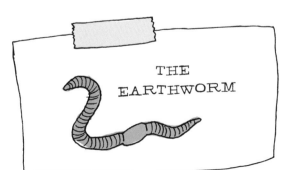

THE EARTHWORM

Describe an earthworm

Pretend you just discovered an earthworm and this is your first time seeing one. What adjectives would you use to describe it? Write them here:

_____   _____   _____

_____   _____   _____

YUM YUM DIET FUN

Match the animal to what it eats by drawing a line from the left column to the right column.

THIS ANIMAL...   EATS THIS.

NOISES AT NIGHT

Nocturnal animals are most active at night. Do you know what sounds they make in the dark? Draw a line from the animal to its sound.

I SPY WITH MY LITTLE EYE...

Check off the plants, animals, and minerals you have seen with your own eyes.

red fox

swan

bison

ant

butterfly

jellyfish

bald eagle

bull thistle

opossum

common butter-cup

crane fly

seal

toad

chickadee

mushroom

honeybee

frog

chrysalis

turtle

black pine sawyer

trillium

moss

striped skunk

mussel

river otter

sycamore bark

cicada

oak leaf

crab

raccoon

king-fisher

coyote

fern

bird nest

prairie dog

caterpillar

sea lion

quartz

red squirrel

skate egg case

tick

seagull

dragonfly

deer

bumblebee

earthworm

lichen

seaweed

Animal Abilities

What kind of animal would you like to be? Read about the different abilities of each pair of animals. Draw a circle around the one you choose.

A grasshopper can leap up to 20 times the length of its body.

A pronghorn antelope sprints at speeds as fast as 55 mph.

A northern flying squirrel jumps from trees to glide away from danger.

A badger can dig itself into a hiding place within moments to escape from a threat.

A California condor has a 10-foot wingspan and can float for hours high in the sky.

A tiny hummingbird flaps its wings up to 80 times per second and can even fly backward.

A skunk defends itself by spraying an attacker with stinky, oily fluid from a gland under its tail.

A porcupine's sharp quills are loosely attached, leaving potential predators with a mouthful of barbs instead of a meal.

An eastern newt can regenerate lost or damaged limbs, and even its eyes and some internal organs.

A western rattlesnake adds a warning rattle to its tail every time it sheds its skin.

Or write here the animal ability you would most like to have:

_____

MAKE IT:
CREATE YOUR OWN BEAVER LODGE

Beavers transform their surroundings by building dams across streams, creating ponds and marshes. These large rodents can cut down sizeable trees with their powerful teeth and jaws. They use sticks and mud to build big lodges with underwater entrances where they shelter in the winter and raise their young.

To create a mini beaver lodge of your own, you'll need to go outside and collect a pile of thin sticks and twigs, along with some dried grass and small leaves.

What You'll Need:
- small sticks and twigs, grasses, leaves
- a piece of cardboard, at least 9x12 inches
- a sheet of blue or green paper (or markers or paint)
- scissors
- white glue
- markers or crayons

1. Cut the colored paper as needed to fit across the bottom of the cardboard to make a pond. Glue it in place. Or you can color in the pond with paint or markers.

2. Draw the outline of a beaver lodge in a cross-section, as shown. That way you can see how the beavers build a platform inside where they can be warm and dry. Add a beaver family using the lodge.

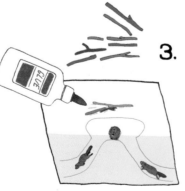

3. Glue sticks, twigs, grass, and leaves around the outline of the lodge, filling in all the spaces.

PUT IN A GOOD WORD

Read the clues and fill in the blanks in the crossword puzzle. Work back and forth between the puzzle and the clues to figure out the answers that you don't know. Some clues have pictures to help you out.

Across

1. The top of a mushroom...or what you might wear on your head
4. Swamp wader
8. If you see these clouds, you might want to grab an umbrella ———→
11. The part of a tree you could easily hug
13. It has about 30,000 sharp quills
14. Dam and lodge builders
17. The female sometimes bites off the head of her mate
18. Every single one is unique (and cold!)
19. The most common mineral on the earth (Hint: It might be in your drinking glass right now.)
20. They pack food into their expandable cheeks
23. You might see this covering a rock

Down

2. They can grow up to an inch a day but shed annually
3. How much wood could a _____ chuck if a _____ could chuck wood?
5. The tallest living trees are part of this subfamily
6. It's colorful and shaped like an arc but hard to catch
7. Tiny droplets of water suspended in the air
9. The process by which a caterpillar becomes a butterfly
10. The underground network of fungus
12. You may hear a buzzing when one flies by
15. They use ultrasonic sounds to find their prey

16. It's red and calls "birdie-birdie-birdie"
20. The thinnest of the layers of the earth, or what you might cut off your sandwiches
21. The hot liquid under the earth's surface
22. Be careful not to be sprayed by one of these

BIRD'S-EYE VIEW

COMMON
YELLOW-THROAT

BLACKBIRD
CHICKADEE
CROW
FALCON
FINCH
FLYCATCHER
GULL
HAWK
HERON
HUMMINGBIRD
JAY
KESTREL
KINGFISHER
NUTHATCH
OWL
PLOVER
SANDPIPER
SPARROW
SWALLOW
TERN
WOODPECKER

There are 21 bird names hidden in this word search. How many can you find? Search vertically, horizontally, and diagonally. Circle each one you find, then cross it off the list.

WHITE-BREASTED
NUTHATCH

```
                                    B  S
                                    Z  C  G  F
                                       T  R  U  W  E
                                    E  N  K  L  M  J
                                 V  K  U  A  M  L  H  A  W  K
                           O  W  I  T  H  E  R  O  N
                        L  C  S  N  H  Y  D  Z
                     P  S  H  A  G  A  F  N
                  B  N  R  I  N  F  T  L  D
               C  D  E  O  C  D  I  C  Y  J
            Q  T  K  W  W  K  P  S  H  C  C
         Y  M  C  O  H  L  A  I  H  I  A  R
         X  E  R  M  U  S  D  P  E  K  T  O
      P  P  R  B  P  M  U  E  E  R  H  C  W
      D  A  F  D  B  M  D  E  R  O  B  H  C
      O  P  W  R  W  D  I  F  I  N  C  H  E
      O  S  F  I  G  N  K  N  T  S  L  H  G  R
   W  N  M  B  G  R  H  O  G  D  W  R  V  G
   H  O  L  K  O  E  E  E  T  B  S  A  Z  U
   H  C  E  C  M  T  J  Q  E  F  I  Q  L  C
   Y  L  R  A  O                 R     L
   H  A  T  L  B                 D     O
   Q  F  S  B  L                 O     W
   D  R  E  Y  M                 G     N
   G  K  A  X                    S     Y
   C  J  I                       A     Z
```

BARRED
OWL

BE A BIRDWATCHER

Can you identify all the birds below? Their names may help you figure it out. Draw a line from the name to the bird.

Red-Winged Blackbird

Mountain Bluebird

Ruby-Throated Hummingbird

Scarlet Tanager

Yellow-Throated Warbler

Eastern Screech Owl

Scissor-Tailed Flycatcher

Red-Tailed Hawk

Useful Beaks

Bird beaks come in many shapes and sizes, each suited for a specific task.
Use the clues below to figure out which task each beak is designed to do.
Draw a line from the clue to the bird.

RED CROSSBILL

RUBY-THROATED HUMMINGBIRD

BALD EAGLE

RINGED KINGFISHER

SPOONBILL

WHITE-THROATED SPARROW

MALLARD DUCK

Long and flat for sweeping through water to find prey, then snapping shut to capture it

Broad and short for skimming through shallow water for plants

A sharp wedge shape for diving into water to catch fish without making a splash

Short, strong hooks for prying apart pinecones to get at the seeds

Very sharp and hooked for tearing up prey

Long and thin for probing into flowers for nectar

Thick and pointed for crushing seeds or catching insects

MAKE IT:
FOLD A PAPER ORIGAMI FOX

Red Fox

The word origami comes from Japanese: oru (to fold) and kami (paper). Try folding a piece of paper to look like a red fox.

1. Make sure your paper is square-shaped. If available, use a red or orange piece of paper.

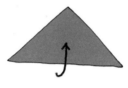

2. Fold the paper in half diagonally.

3. Fold the bottom right corner to the top.

4. Fold the bottom left corner to meet it.

5. Flip the paper over.

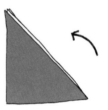

6. Fold the right point to the left.

7. Rotate the paper counterclockwise.

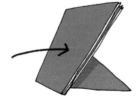

8. Fold the paper slightly diagonally to the right.

9. Let the flaps open.

10. Fold down the middle piece to make a face, and draw on its features.

SECRET CODE

Using the code above, can you decipher the message below?

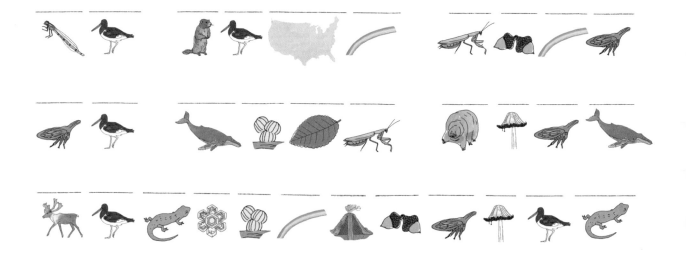

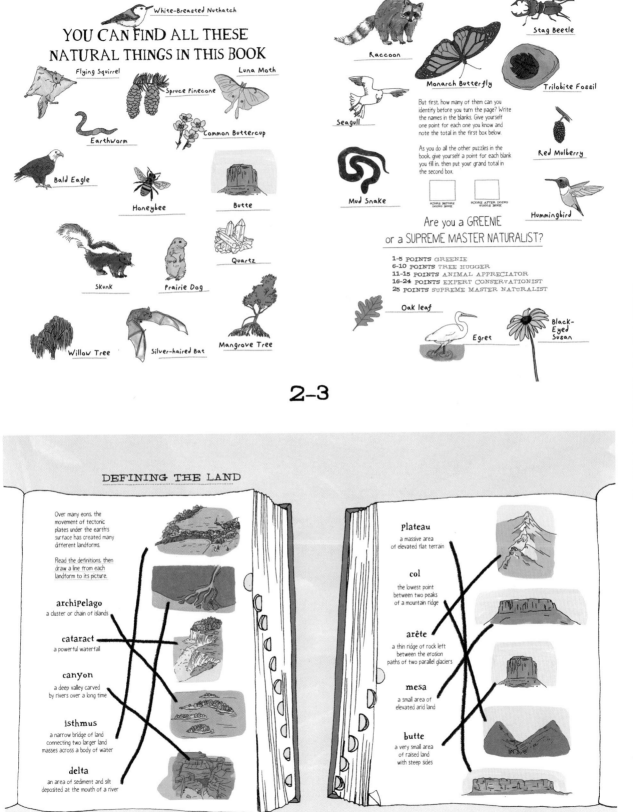

YOU CAN FIND ALL THESE NATURAL THINGS IN THIS BOOK

White-Breasted Nuthatch

Flying Squirrel

Spruce Pinecone

Luna Moth

Earthworm

Common Buttercup

Bald Eagle

Honeybee

Butte

Skunk

Prairie Dog

Quartz

Willow Tree

Silver-haired Bat

Mangrove Tree

Raccoon

Monarch Butterfly

Stag Beetle

Trilobite Fossil

Seagull

Mud Snake

Red Mulberry

Hummingbird

But first, how many of them can you identify before you turn the page? Write the names in the blanks. Give yourself one point for each one you know and note the total in the first box below.

As you do all the other puzzles in the book, give yourself a point for each blank you fill in, then put your grand total in the second box.

SCORE BEFORE DOING BOOK

SCORE AFTER DOING WHOLE BOOK

Are you a GREENIE or a SUPREME MASTER NATURALIST?

1-5 POINTS GREENIE
6-10 POINTS TREE HUGGER
11-15 POINTS ANIMAL APPRECIATOR
16-24 POINTS EXPERT CONSERVATIONIST
25 POINTS SUPREME MASTER NATURALIST

Oak leaf

Egret

Black-Eyed Susan

ANSWER KEY

DEFINING THE LAND

Over many eons, the movement of tectonic plates under the earth's surface has created many different landforms.

Read the definitions, then draw a line from each landform to its picture.

archipelago
a cluster or chain of islands

cataract
a powerful waterfall

canyon
a deep valley carved by rivers over a long time

isthmus
a narrow bridge of land connecting two larger land masses across a body of water

delta
an area of sediment and silt deposited at the mouth of a river

plateau
a massive area of elevated flat terrain

col
the lowest point between two peaks of a mountain ridge

arête
a thin ridge of rock left between the erosion paths of two parallel glaciers

mesa
a small area of elevated arid land

butte
a very small area of raised land with steep sides

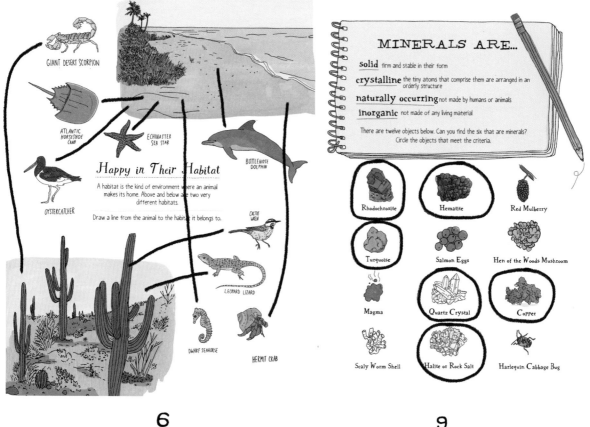

Happy in Their Habitat

A habitat is the kind of environment where an animal makes its home. Above and below are two very different habitats.

Draw a line from the animal to the habitat it belongs to.

GIANT DESERT SCORPION

ATLANTIC HORSESHOE CRAB

ECHINASTER SEA STAR

OYSTERCATCHER

BOTTLENOSE DOLPHIN

CACTUS WREN

LEOPARD LIZARD

DWARF SEAHORSE

HERMIT CRAB

6

MINERALS ARE...

solid firm and stable in their form

crystalline the tiny atoms that comprise them are arranged in an orderly structure

naturally occurring not made by humans or animals

inorganic not made of any living material

There are twelve objects below. Can you find the six that are minerals? Circle the objects that meet the criteria.

Rhodochrosite

Hematite

Red Mulberry

Turquoise

Salmon Eggs

Hen of the Woods Mushroom

Magma

Quartz Crystal

Copper

Scaly Worm Shell

Halite or Rock Salt

Harlequin Cabbage Bug

9

BINOCULAR EYES

Pretend you are using binoculars to look at the creatures and plants that live in and around a pond. Draw a line from the details in the circles to where you find them in the larger picture.

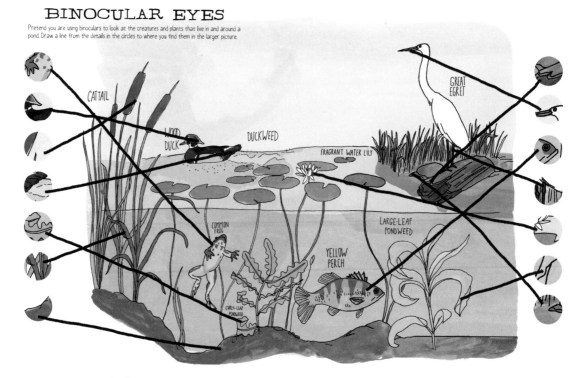

CATTAIL

GREAT EGRET

WOOD DUCK

DUCKWEED

FRAGRANT WATER LILY

COMMON FROG

LARGE-LEAF PONDWEED

YELLOW PERCH

CURLY-LEAF PONDWEED

12

13

Let It Snow

Can you fill in the 4 X 4 grid below, so all the letters of the word S-N-O-W appear in each row and column only once?

		W	
			O
S			
	W		N

If you look closely, all these snowflakes are different except one pair. Can you find and circle the two snowflakes that are exactly the same?

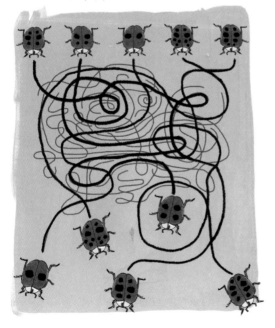

17

COLORFUL FLOWER NAMES

Combine the circled letters from these flower names to spell the colorful parts of a flower that attract pollinators.

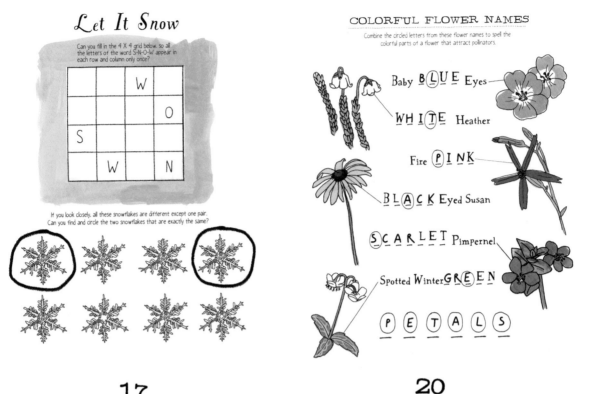

Baby B[L]U E Eyes

WH I[T]E Heather

Fire [P]I N K

B L[A]C K Eyed Susan

[S]C[A]R L E T Pimpernel

Spotted Winter G R[E]E N

[P] E T[A] L[S]

20

LADYBUG LANES

Follow each ladybug on its winding journey through the grass. When you find the corresponding ladybug, draw the same number of spots on its back.

21

ANATOMY OF A BEE

Match the body parts in the chart below with the image. Label the image by writing the correct numbers on the lines.

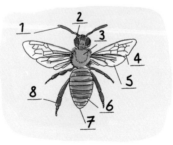

1. antenna - contains thousands of tiny sensors that detect smells
2. compound eye - for all-around vision
3. thorax - segment between the head and abdomen, where the wings attach
4. forewing
5. hind wing } 2-part wings hook together in flight but separate at rest
6. abdomen - contains all the organs, wax glands, and stinger
7. stinger - only present on worker and queen bees
8. leg

22

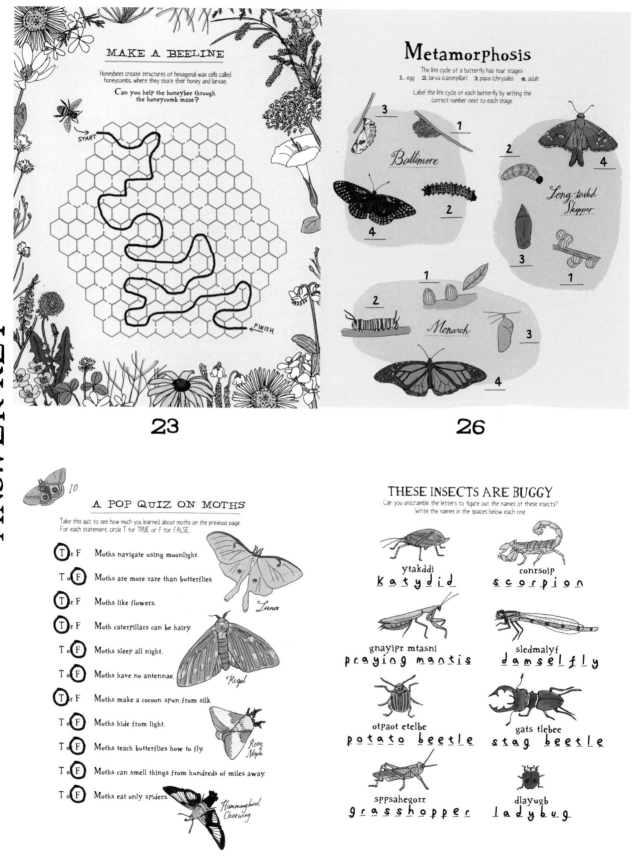

MAKE A BEELINE

Honeybees create structures of hexagonal wax cells called honeycombs, where they store their honey and larvae.

Can you help the honeybee through the honeycomb maze?

START

FINISH

23

Metamorphosis

The life cycle of a butterfly has four stages:
1. egg   2. larva (caterpillar)   3. pupa (chrysalis)   4. adult

Label the life cycle of each butterfly by writing the correct number next to each stage.

Baltimore — 3, 1, 2, 4

Long-tailed Skipper — 2, 4, 3, 1

Monarch — 1, 2, 3, 4

26

A POP QUIZ ON MOTHS

Take this quiz to see how much you learned about moths on the previous page. For each statement, circle T for TRUE or F for FALSE.

T or F   Moths navigate using moonlight.

T or **F**   Moths are more rare than butterflies.

T or F   Moths like flowers.

T or F   Moth caterpillars can be hairy.

T or **F**   Moths sleep all night.

T or **F**   Moths have no antennae.

T or F   Moths make a cocoon spun from silk.

T or **F**   Moths hide from light.

T or **F**   Moths teach butterflies how to fly.

T or **F**   Moths can smell things from hundreds of miles away.

T or **F**   Moths eat only spiders.

Luna

Regal

Rosy Maple

Hummingbird Clearwing

28

THESE INSECTS ARE BUGGY

Can you unscramble the letters to figure out the names of these insects?
Write the names in the spaces below each one.

ytakddi
katydid

conrsoiP
scorpion

gnayipr mtasni
praying mantis

sledmalyf
damselfly

otpaot etelbe
potato beetle

gats tlebee
stag beetle

sppsahegorr
grasshopper

dlayugb
ladybug

31

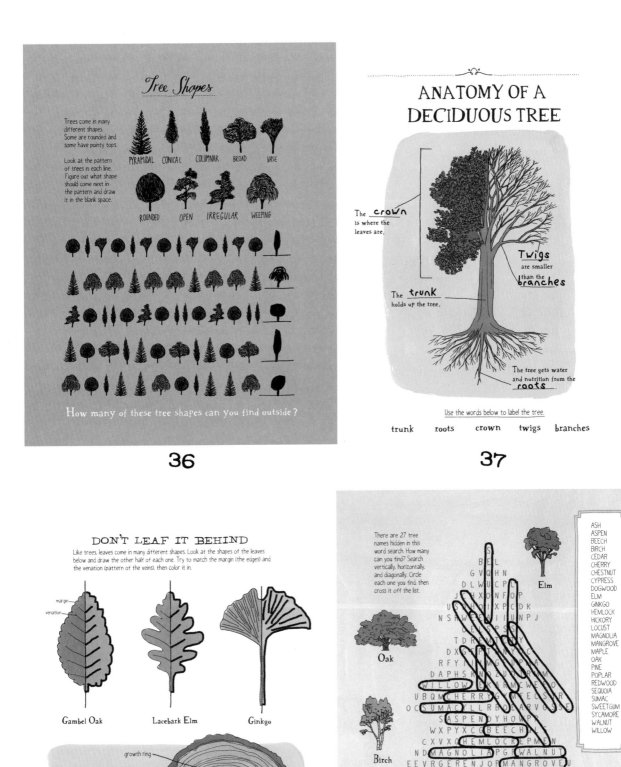

Tree Shapes

Trees come in many different shapes. Some are rounded and some have pointy tops.

Look at the pattern of trees in each line. Figure out what shape should come next in the pattern and draw it in the blank space.

PYRAMIDAL CONICAL COLUMNAR BROAD VASE

ROUNDED OPEN IRREGULAR WEEPING

How many of these tree shapes can you find outside?

36

ANATOMY OF A DECIDUOUS TREE

The **crown** is where the leaves are.

Twigs are smaller than the **branches**

The **trunk** holds up the tree.

The tree gets water and nutrition from the **roots**

Use the words below to label the tree.

trunk   roots   crown   twigs   branches

37

DON'T LEAF IT BEHIND

Like trees, leaves come in many different shapes. Look at the shapes of the leaves below and draw the other half of each one. Try to match the margin (the edges) and the venation (pattern of the veins), then color it in.

margin
venation

Gambel Oak   Lacebark Elm   Ginkgo

HOW OLD WAS THIS TREE?

growth ring

The age of a tree can be determined by counting the growth rings in a cross section of its trunk. Count the rings and write the age of the tree here.

22 years old

38

There are 27 tree names hidden in this word search. How many can you find? Search vertically, horizontally, and diagonally. Circle each one you find, then cross it off the list.

Elm

Oak

Birch

Willow

Mangrove

ASH
ASPEN
BEECH
BIRCH
CEDAR
CHERRY
CHESTNUT
CYPRESS
DOGWOOD
ELM
GINKGO
HEMLOCK
HICKORY
LOCUST
MAGNOLIA
MANGROVE
MAPLE
OAK
PINE
POPLAR
REDWOOD
SEQUOIA
SUMAC
SWEETGUM
SYCAMORE
WALNUT
WILLOW

39

A-MAZING MYCELIUM

Fungi absorb nutrients through vast underground networks of white, branching threads called mycelium. Hidden in the soil, and sometimes mistaken for roots, mycelium is actually the proper body of a fungus.

Now imagine you are the tiniest burrowing insect lost in a maze of mycelium, and try to get through.

START

FINISH

42

What's on that ROTTING LOG?

A dead tree on the forest floor may not look like much, but the decomposing wood hosts a party of plant and animal life.

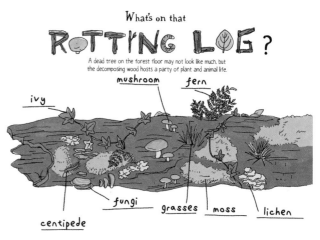

ivy

mushroom

fern

centipede

fungi

grasses

moss

lichen

Use the words below to label what's on the rotting log.

ferns ivy grasses lichen centipede fungi moss mushroom

43

YUM YUM DIET FUN

Match the animal to what it eats by drawing a line from the left column to the right column.

THIS ANIMAL...   EATS THIS.

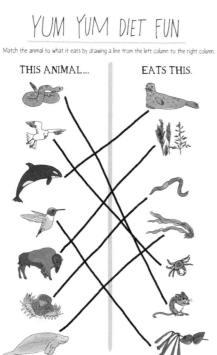

44

NOISES AT NIGHT

Nocturnal animals are most active at night. Do you know what sounds they make in the dark? Draw a line from the animal to its sound.

SQUEAK SQUEAK

CHIT-CHIT CHITTER...

WHO-HOOO HOO...

SSSSSS...

AWOOOOOOOO...

RAWNK RAWNK...

silver haired bat

American green tree frog

mud snake

raccoon

barred owl

gray wolf

45

51

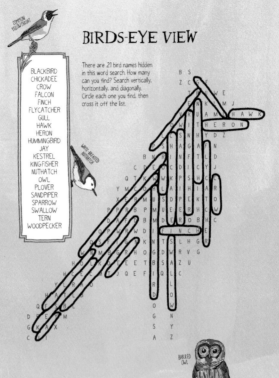

BIRDS-EYE VIEW

There are 21 bird names hidden in this word search. How many can you find? Search vertically, horizontally, and diagonally. Circle each one you find, then cross it off the list.

BLACKBIRD
CHICKADEE
CROW
FALCON
FINCH
FLYCATCHER
GULL
HAWK
HERON
HUMMINGBIRD
JAY
KESTREL
KINGFISHER
NUTHATCH
OWL
PLOVER
SANDPIPER
SPARROW
SWALLOW
TERN
WOODPECKER

52

BE A BIRDWATCHER

Can you identify all the birds below? Their names may help you figure it out. Draw a line from the name to the bird.

Red-Winged Blackbird
Mountain Bluebird
Ruby-Throated Hummingbird
Scarlet Tanager
Yellow-Throated Warbler
Eastern Screech Owl
Scissor-Tailed Flycatcher
Red-Tailed Hawk

53

Useful Beaks

Bird beaks come in many shapes and sizes, each suited for a specific task. Use the clues below to figure out which task each beak is designed to do. Draw a line from the clue to the bird.

Long and flat for sweeping through water to find prey, then snapping shut to capture it

Broad and short for skimming through shallow water for plants

A sharp wedge shape for diving into water to catch fish without making a splash

Short, strong hooks for prying apart pinecones to get at the seeds

Very sharp and hooked for tearing up prey

Long and thin for probing into flowers for nectar

Thick and pointed for crushing seeds or catching insects

54

ANSWER KEY

SECRET CODE

Using the code above, can you decipher the message below?

DO YOUR PART
TO HELP WITH
CONSERVATION

57

Illustrations and text © 2023 by Julia Rothman

Storey books are available at special discounts when purchased in bulk for premiums and sales promotions as well as for fund-raising or educational use. Special editions or book excerpts can also be created to specification. For details, please send an email to special.markets@hbgusa.com.

Storey Publishing
210 MASS MoCA Way
North Adams, MA 01247
storey.com

Storey Publishing, LLC is an imprint of Workman Publishing Co., Inc.,
a subsidiary of Hachette Book Group, Inc.,
1290 Avenue of the Americas, New York, NY 10104

Distributed in Europe by Hachette Livre, 58 rue Jean Bleuzen, 92 178 Vanves Cedex, France
Distributed in the United Kingdom by Hachette Book Group, UK, Carmelite House, 50 Victoria Embankment, London EC4Y 0DZ

ISBN: 978-1-63586-768-8 (paperback)

Printed in China through Asia Pacific Offset
10 9 8 7 6 5 4 3 2 1